The Coloring Studio

Imaginary Cities

Monsieur Dupont

Little, Brown and Company
New York Boston

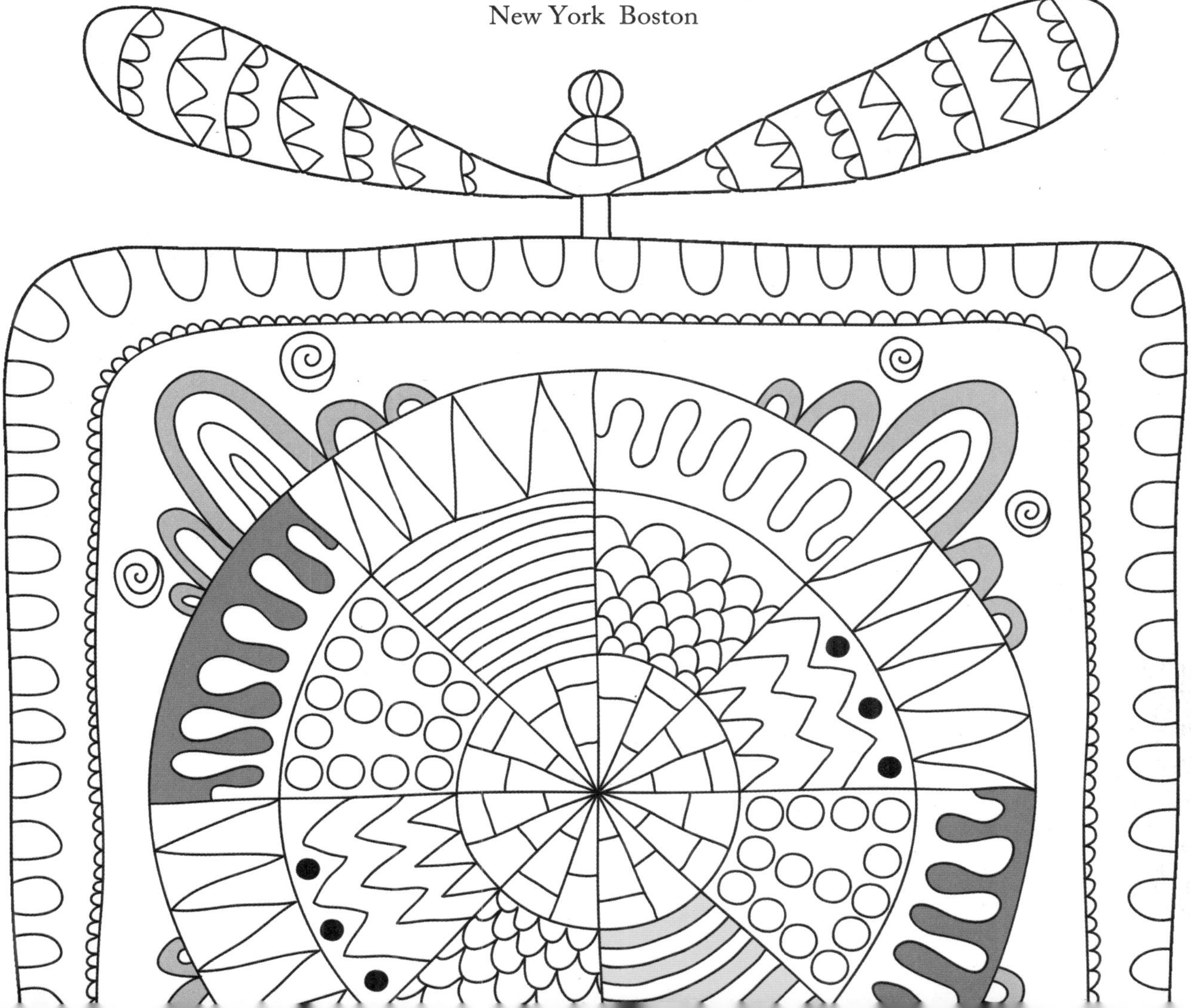

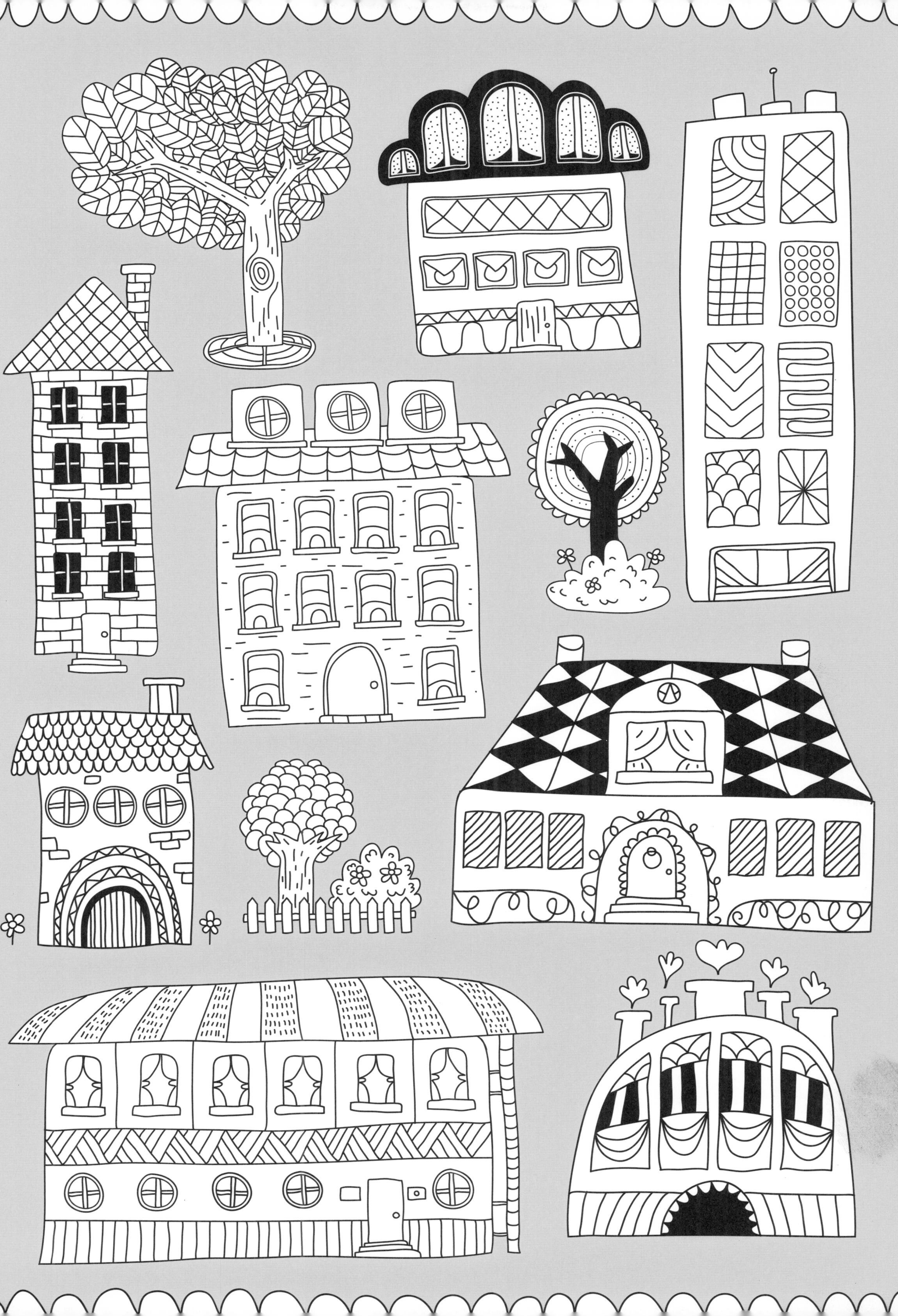

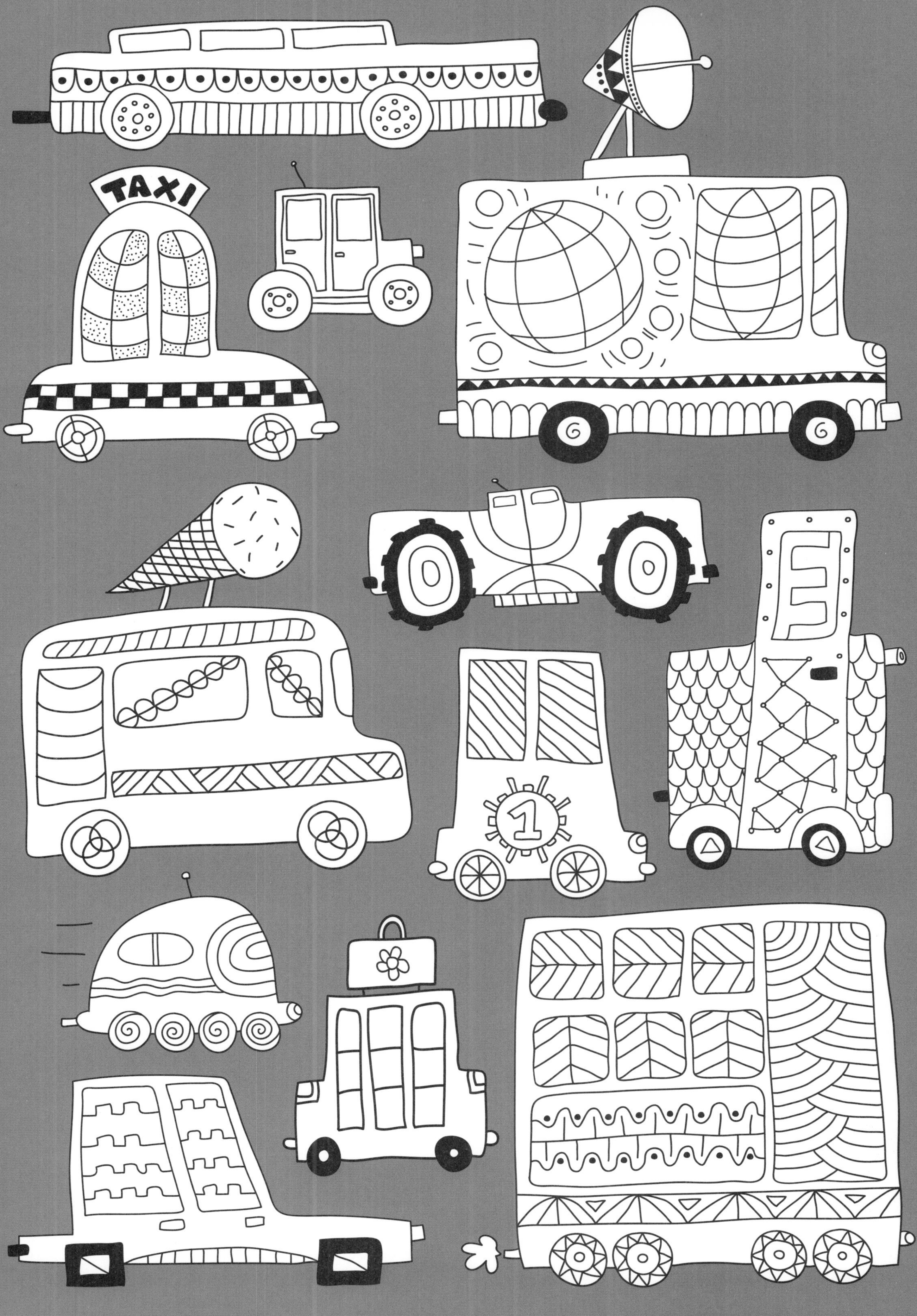
TAXI
1

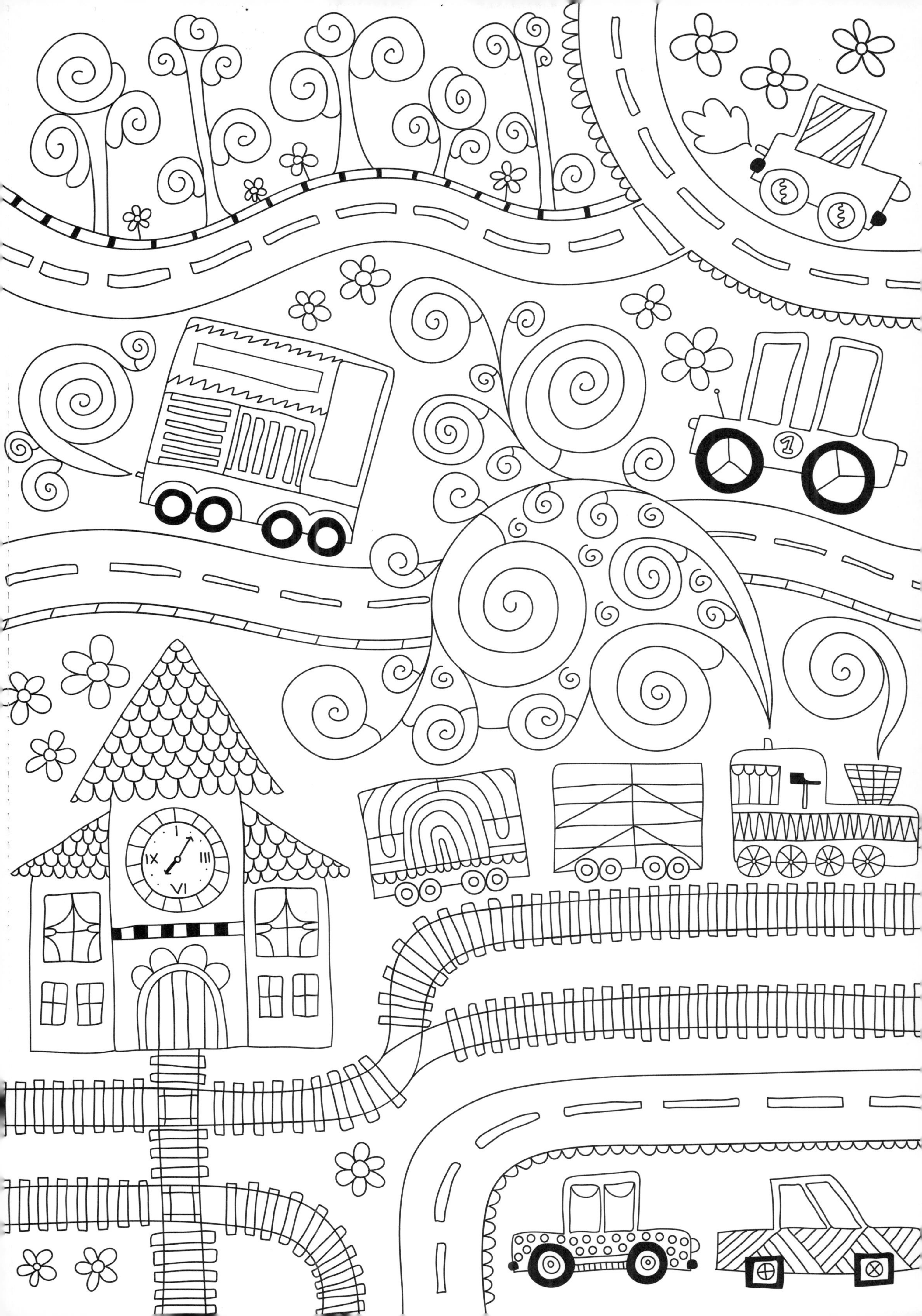
1
I
III
VI
IX

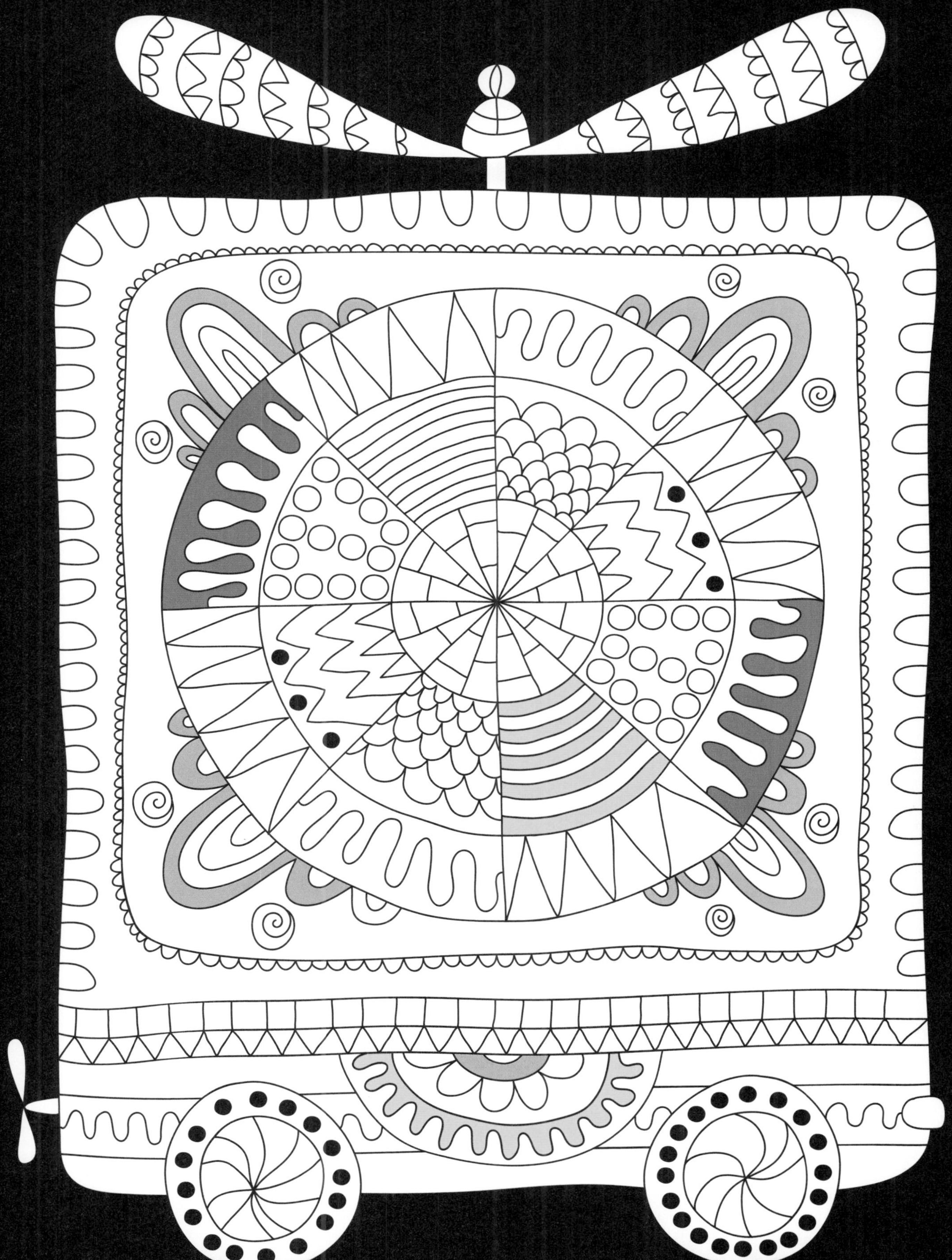

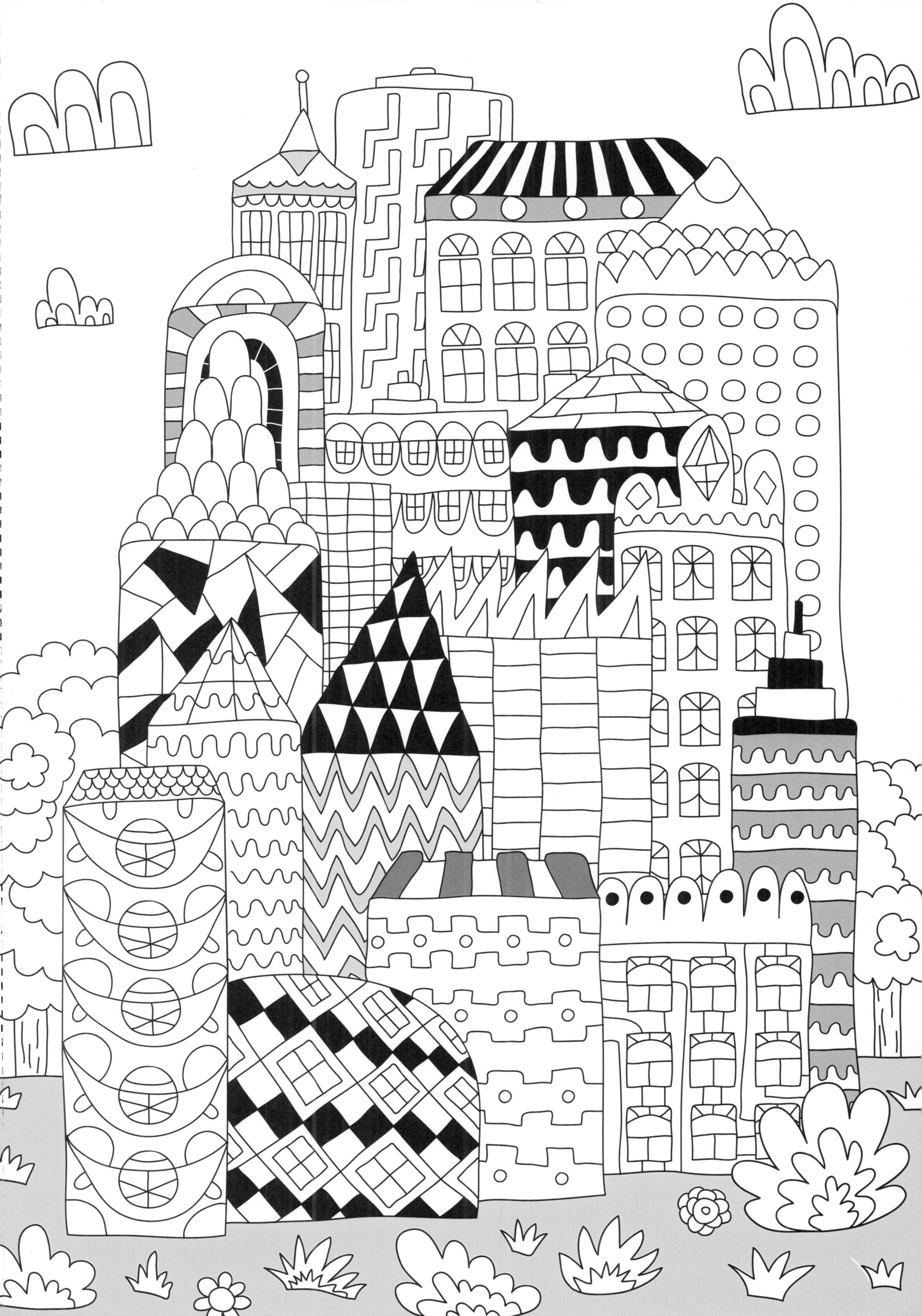

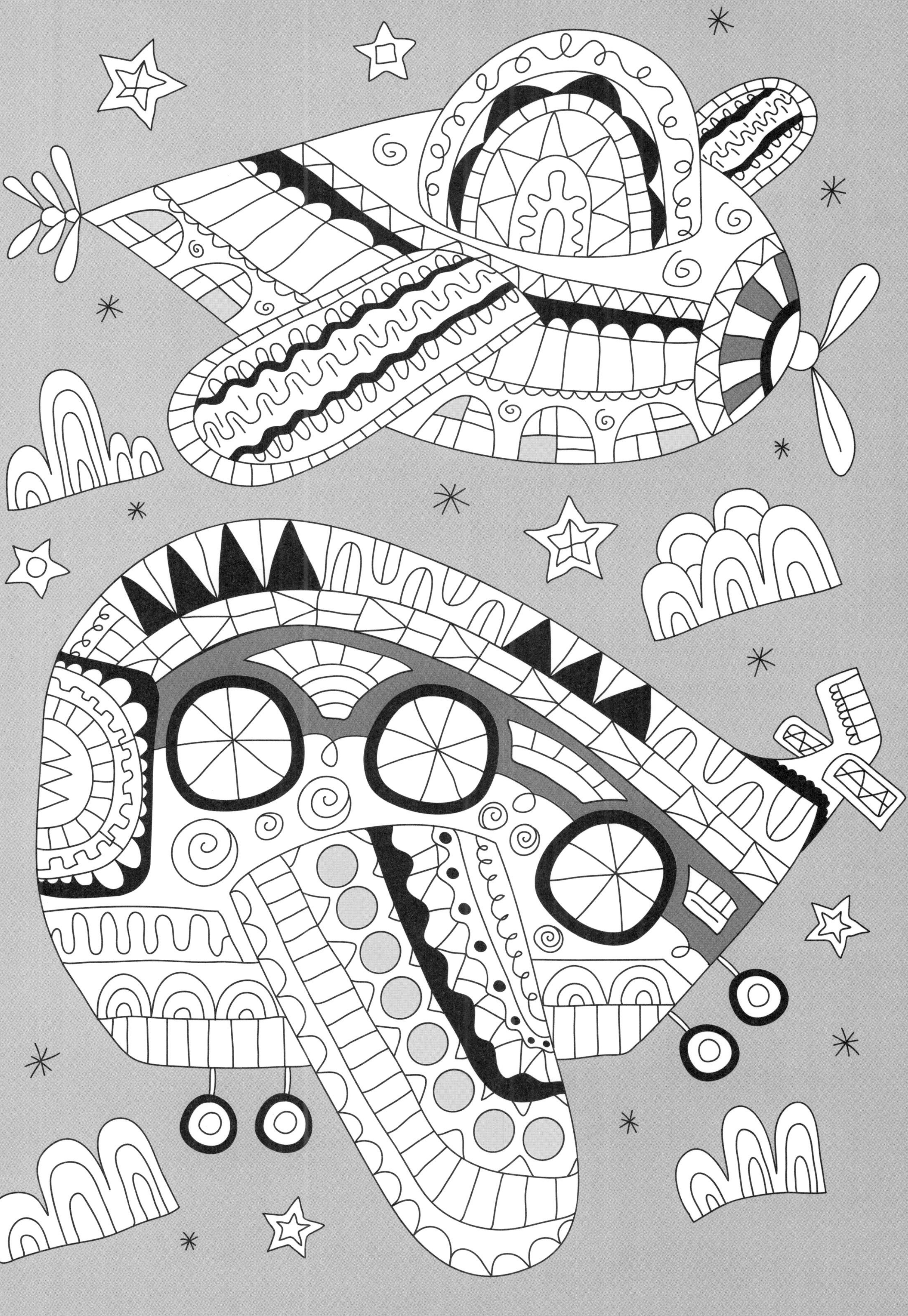

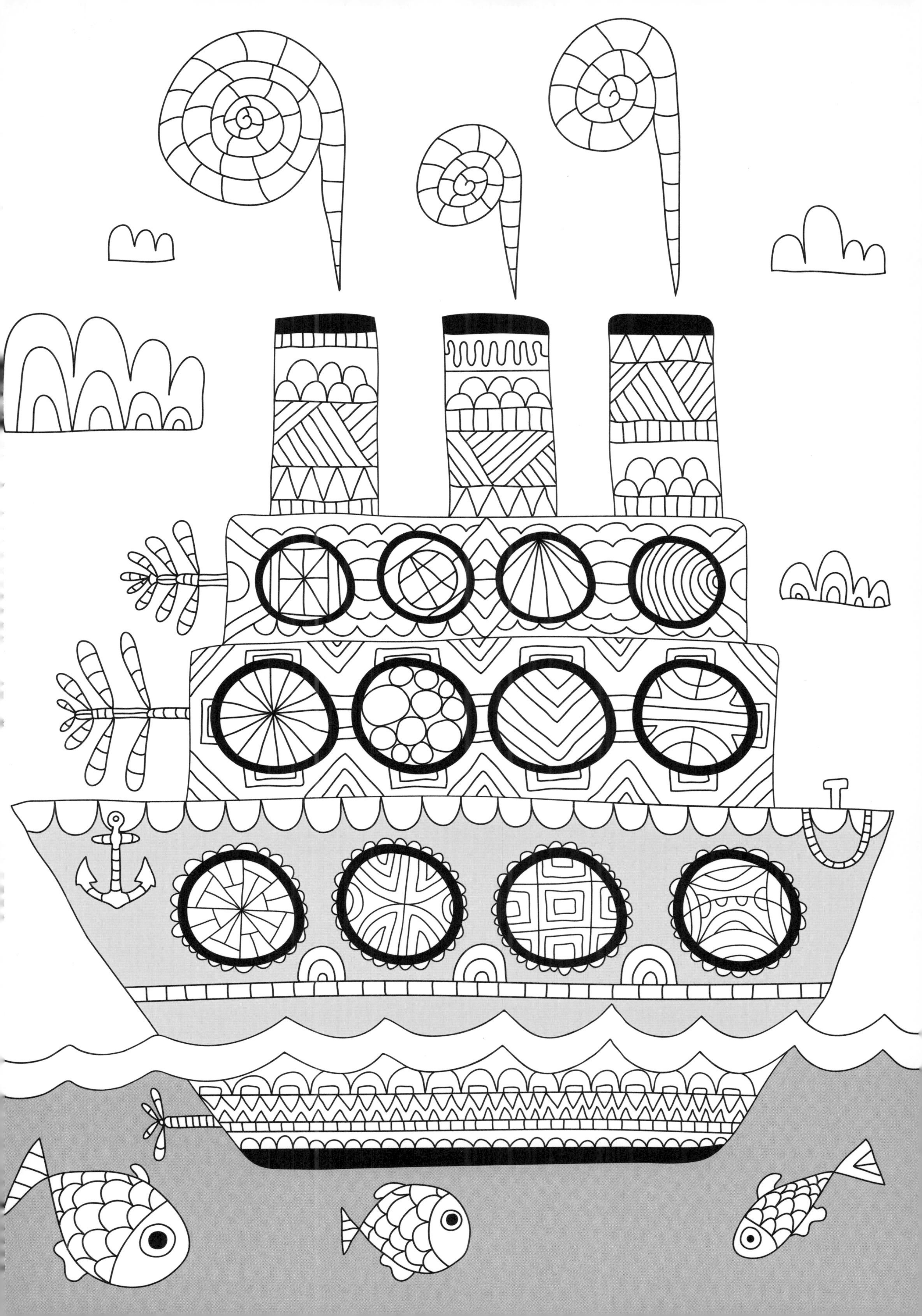

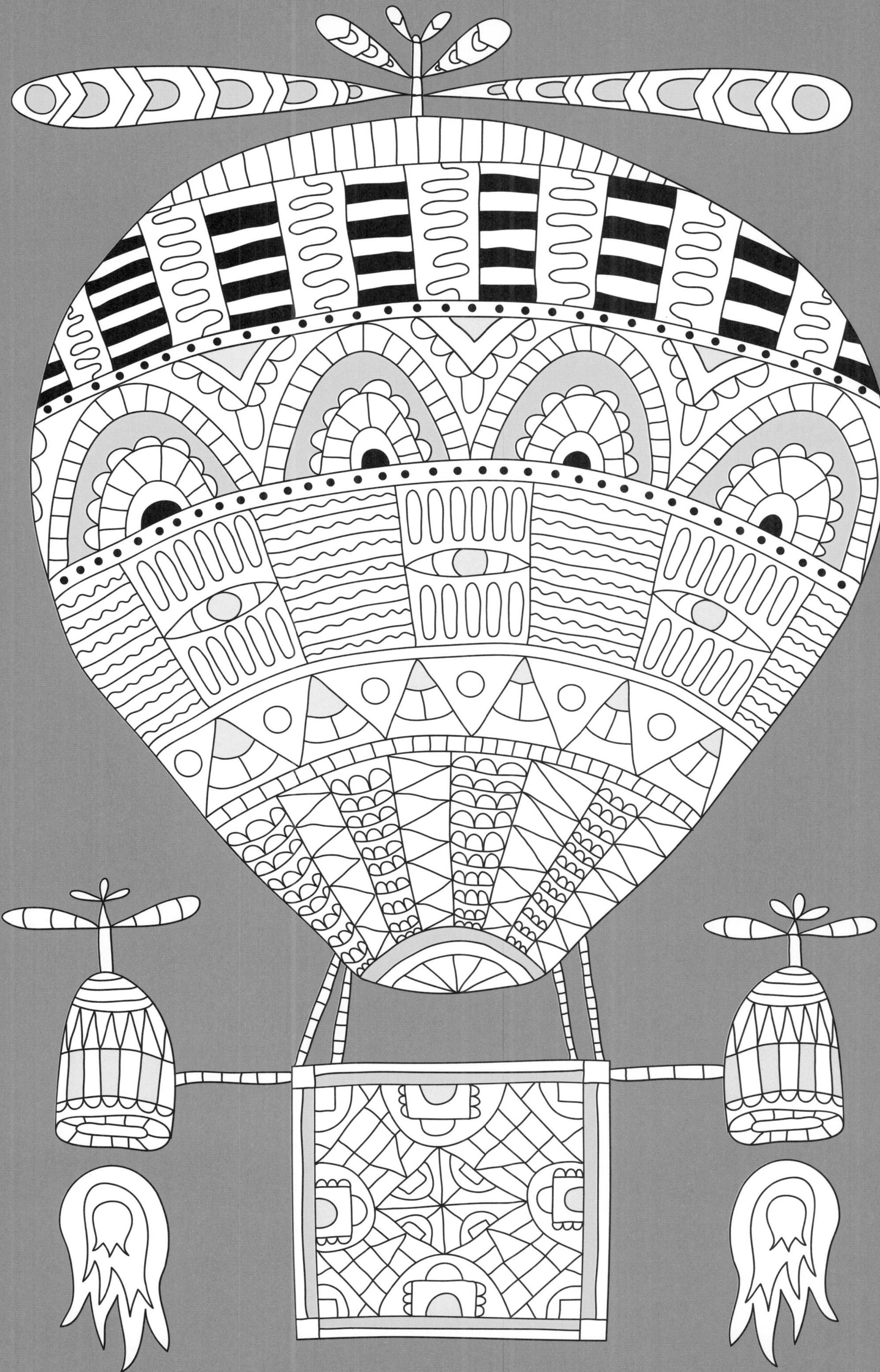

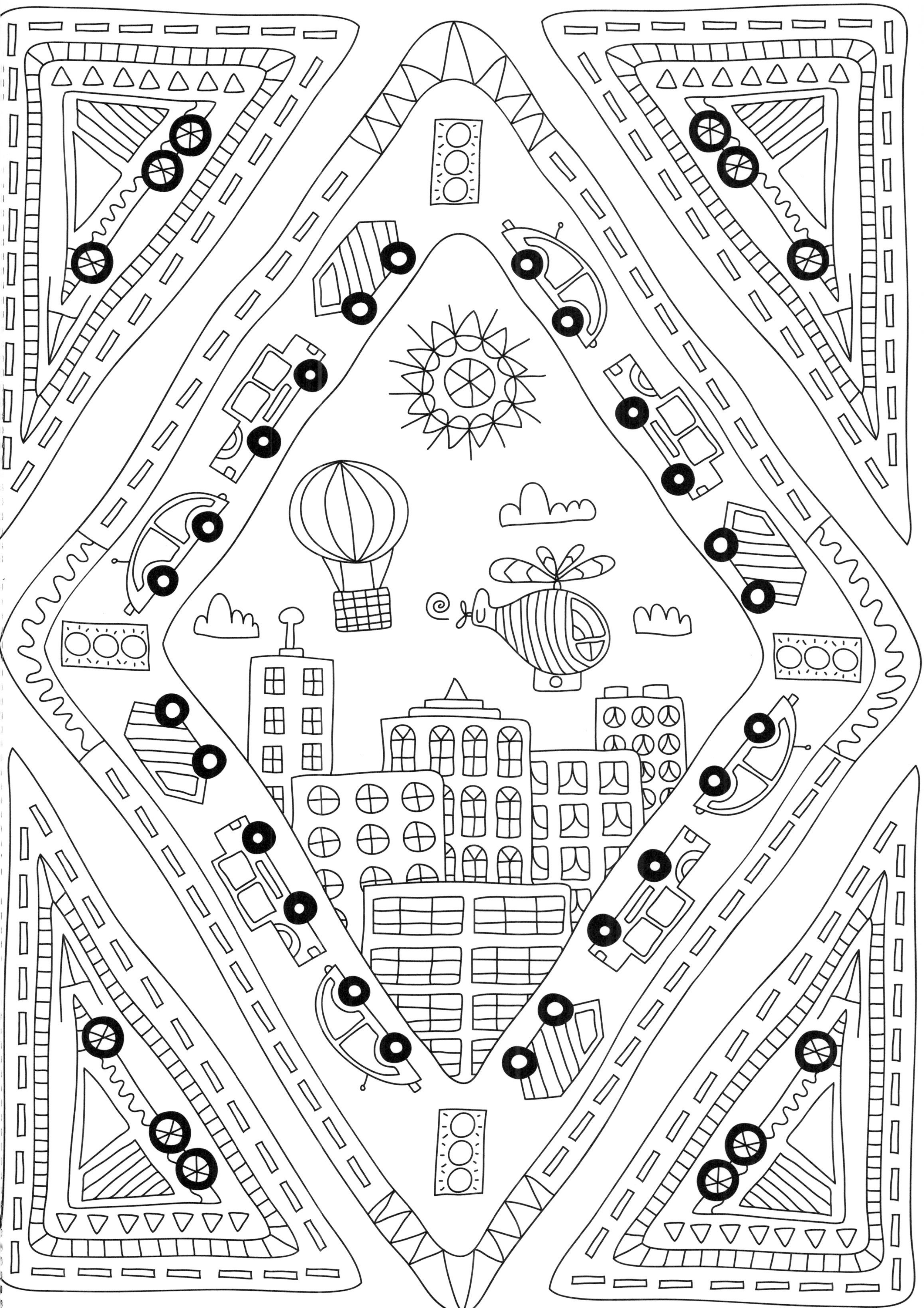

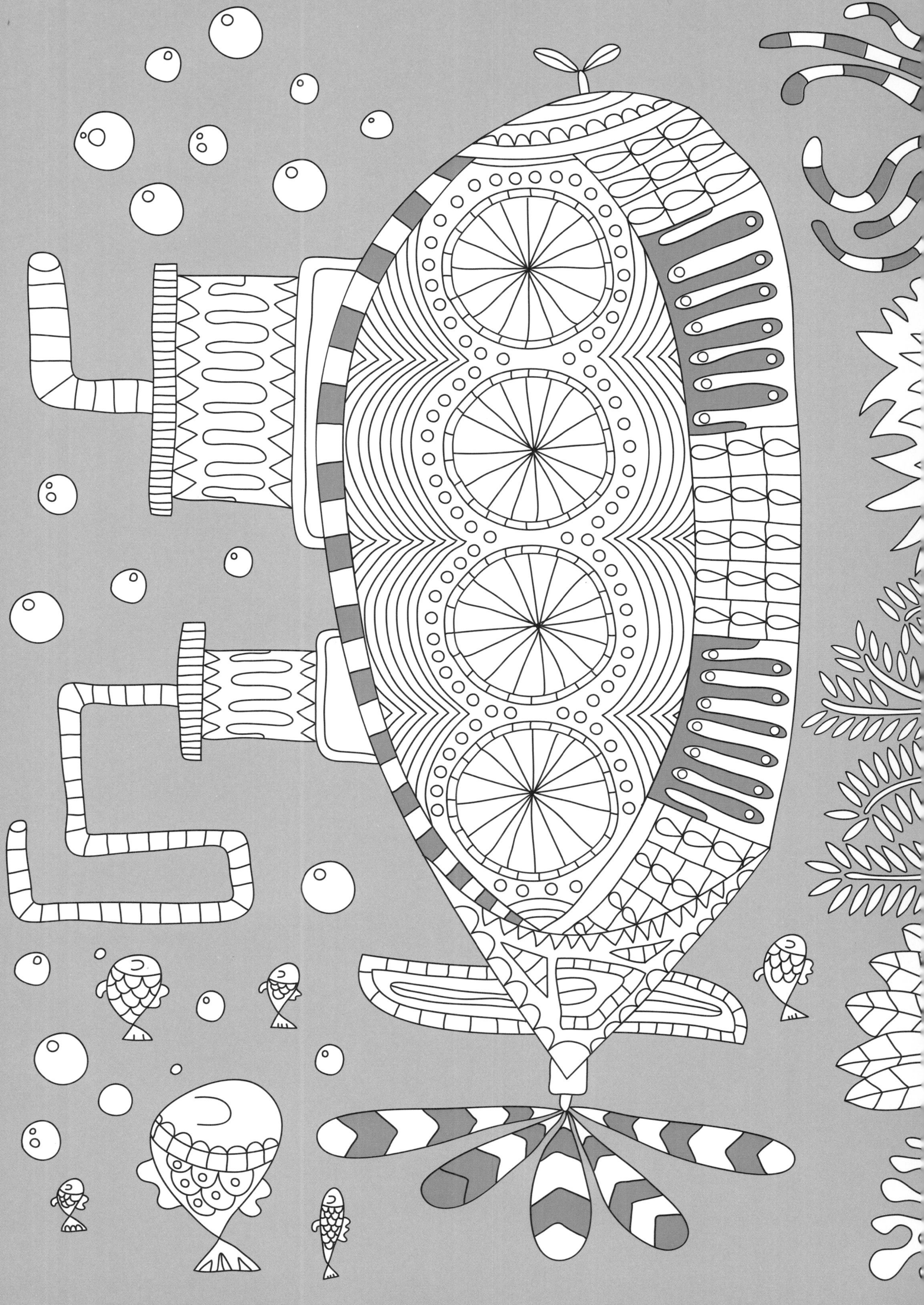

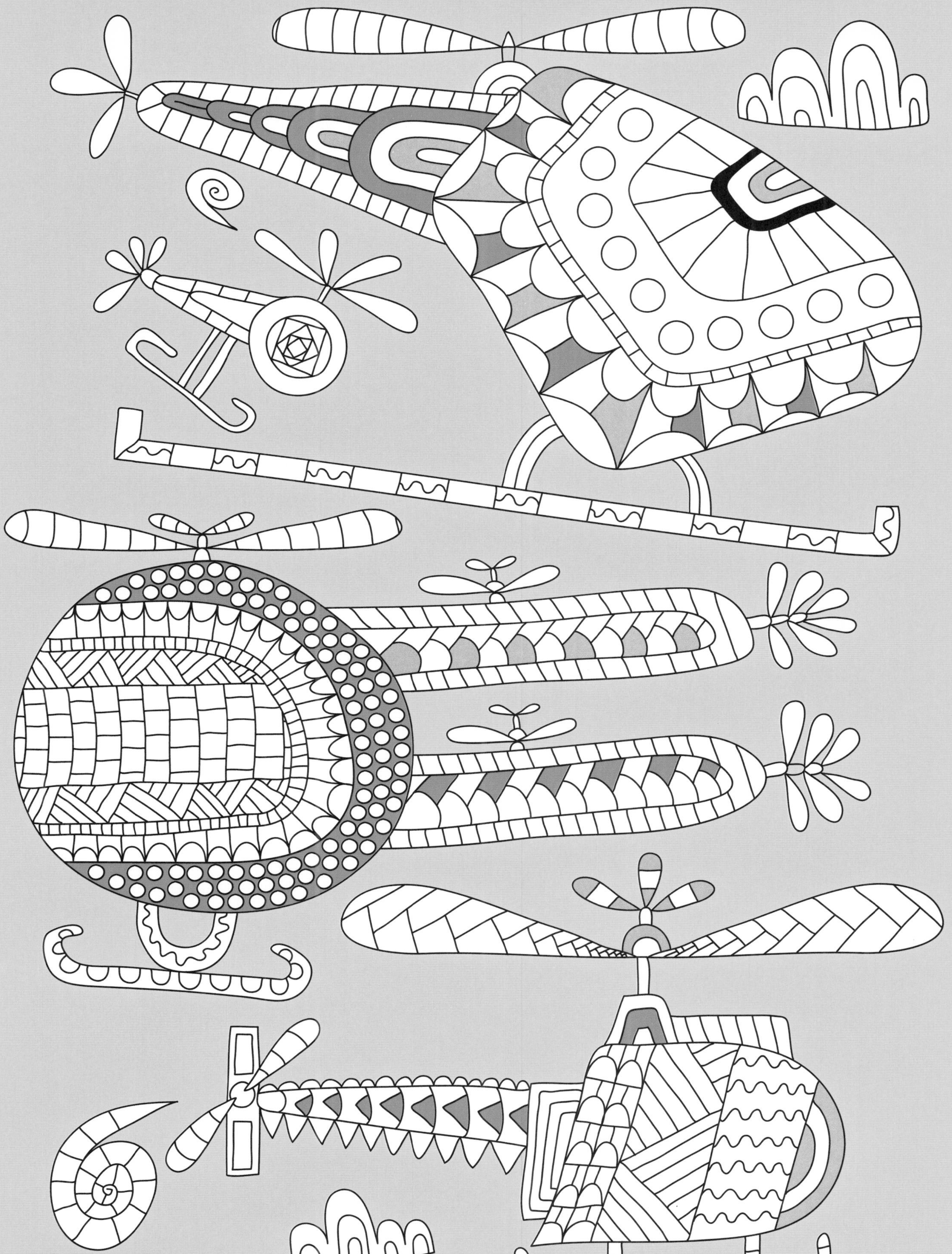

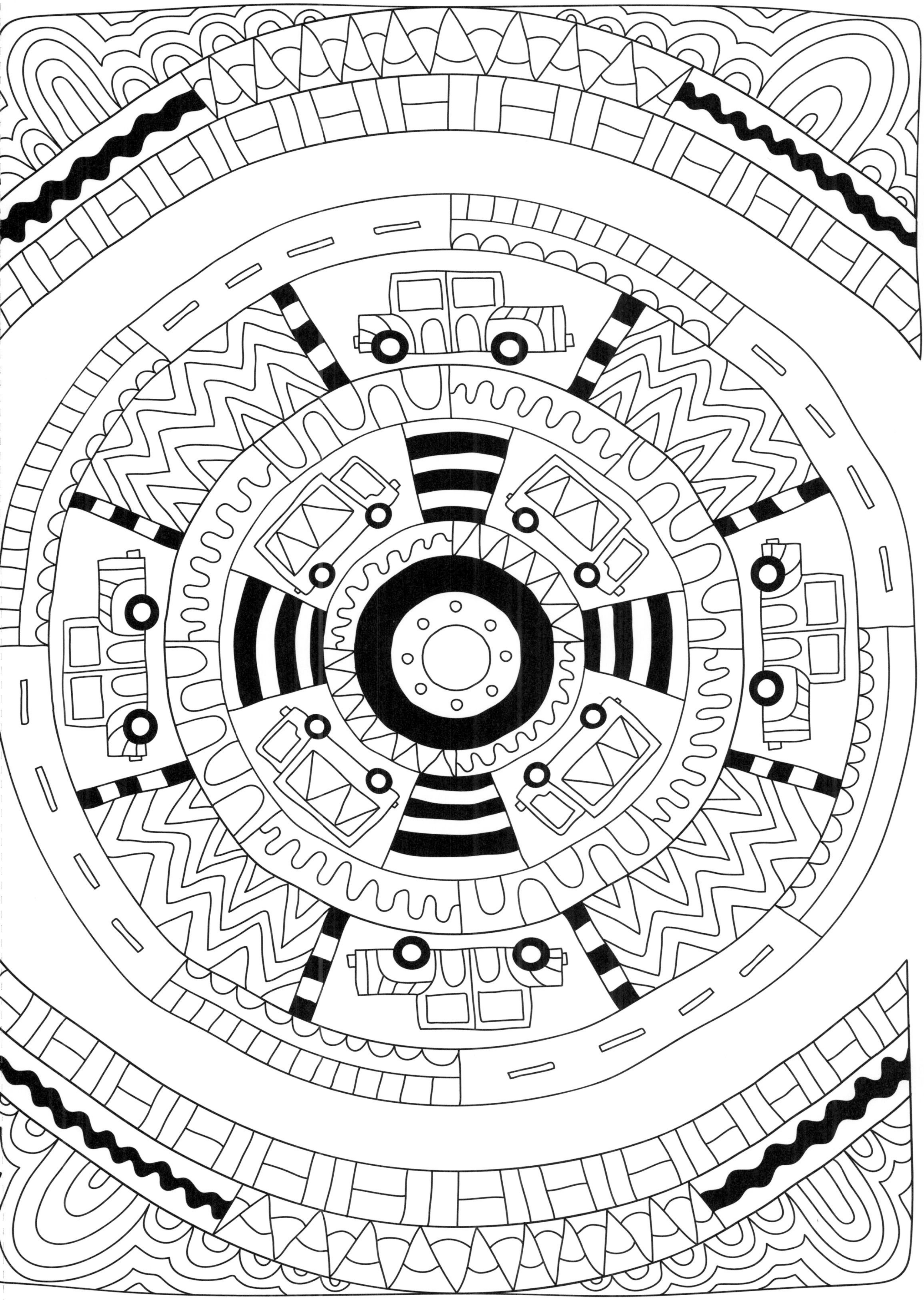

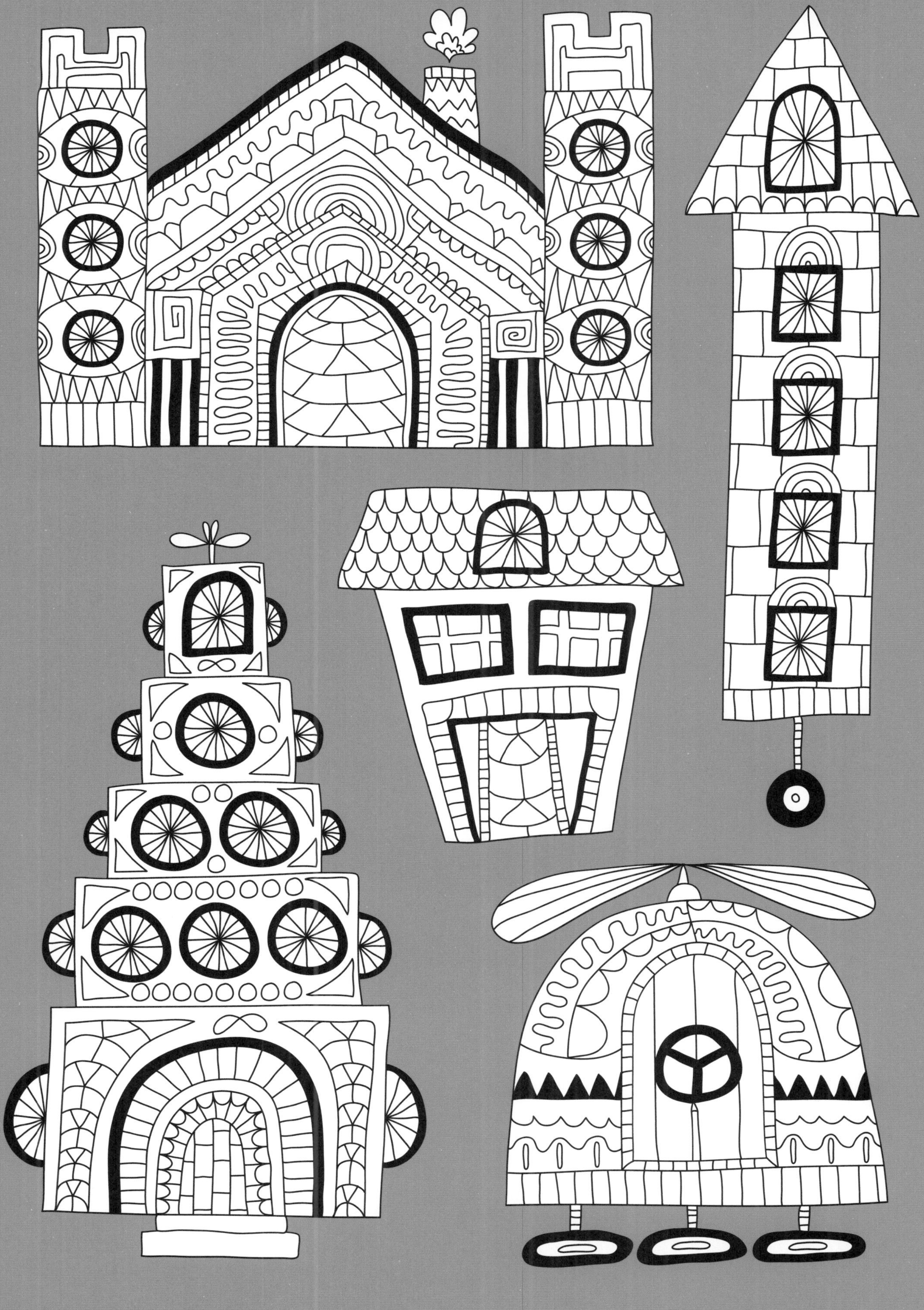

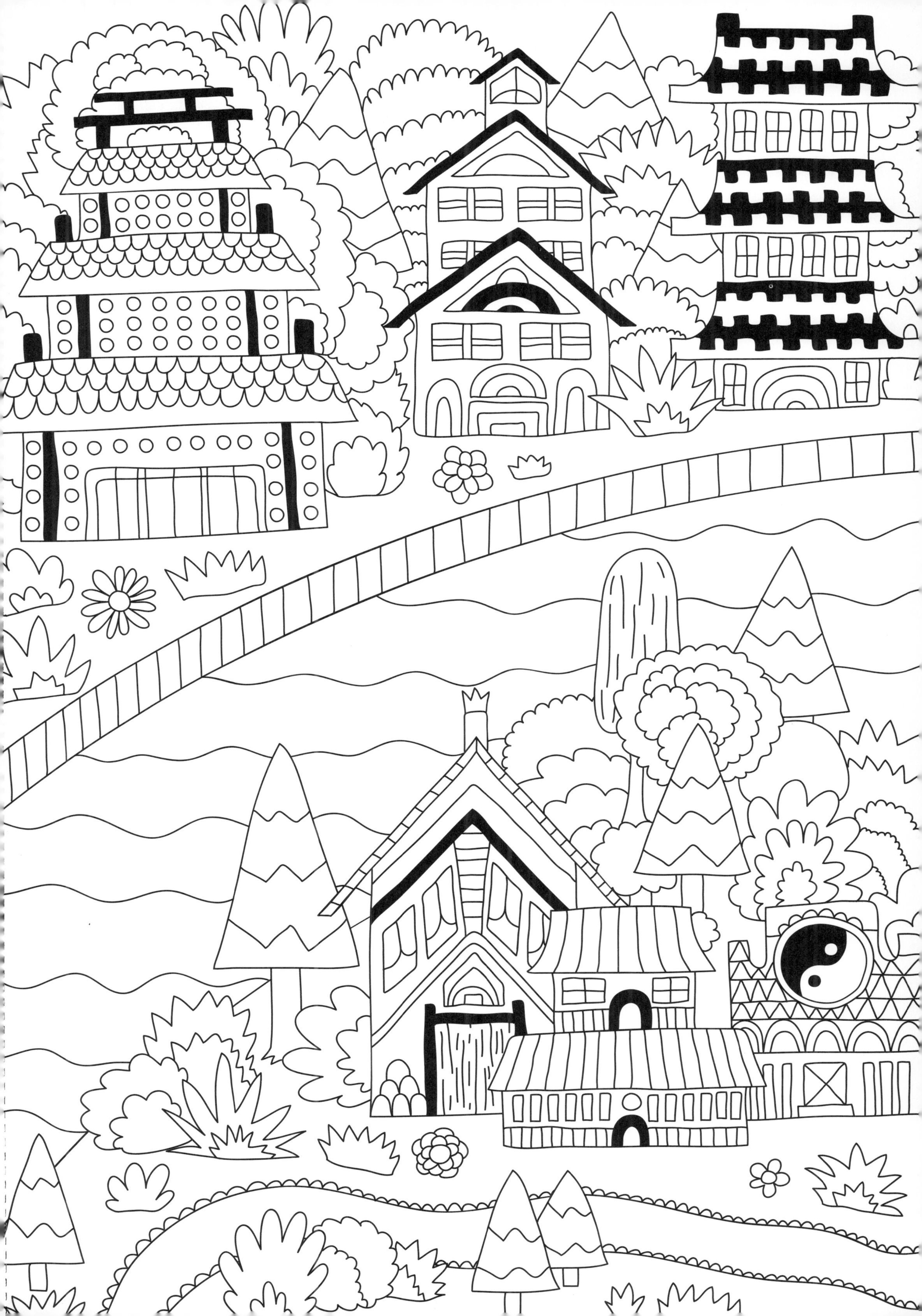

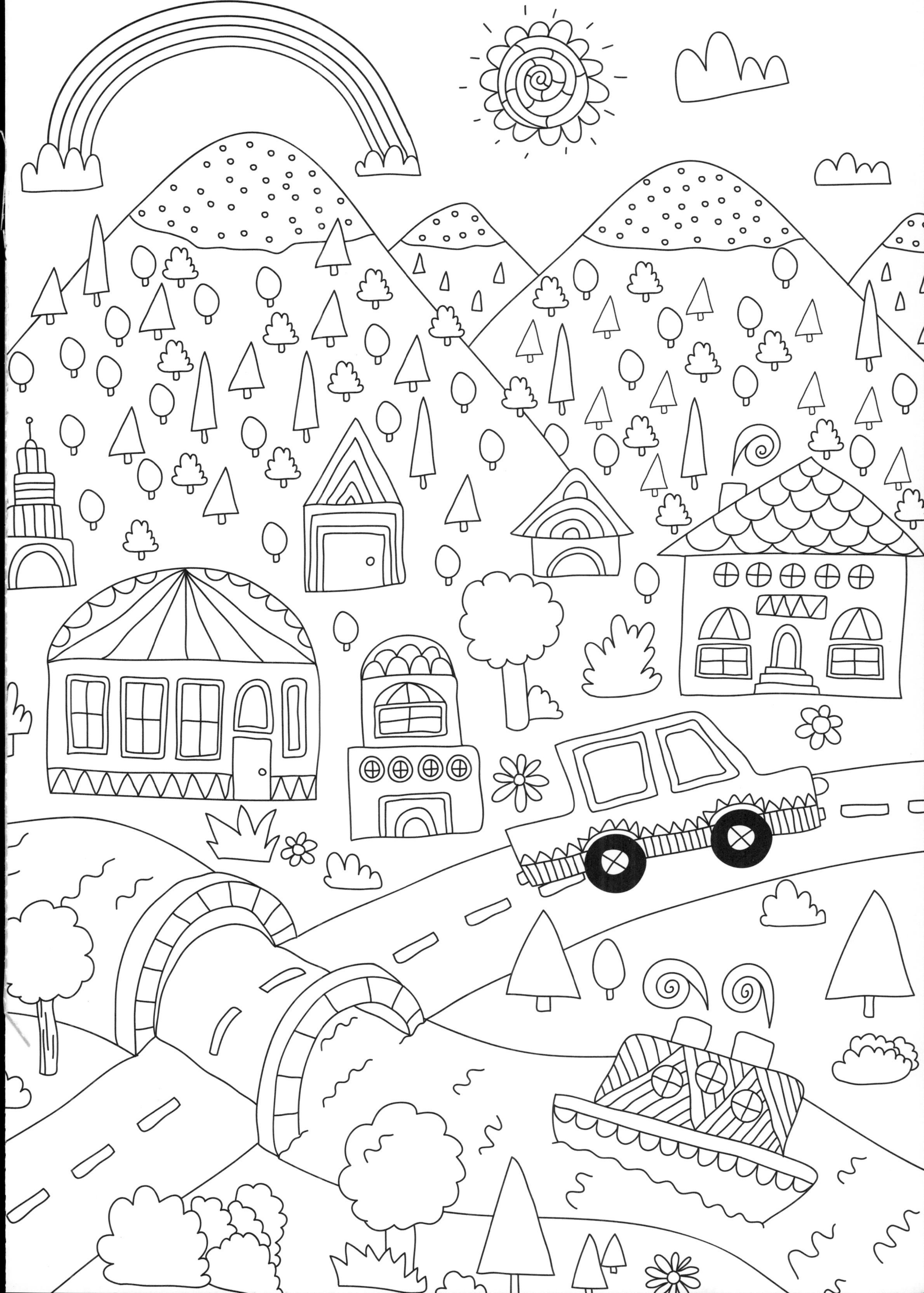

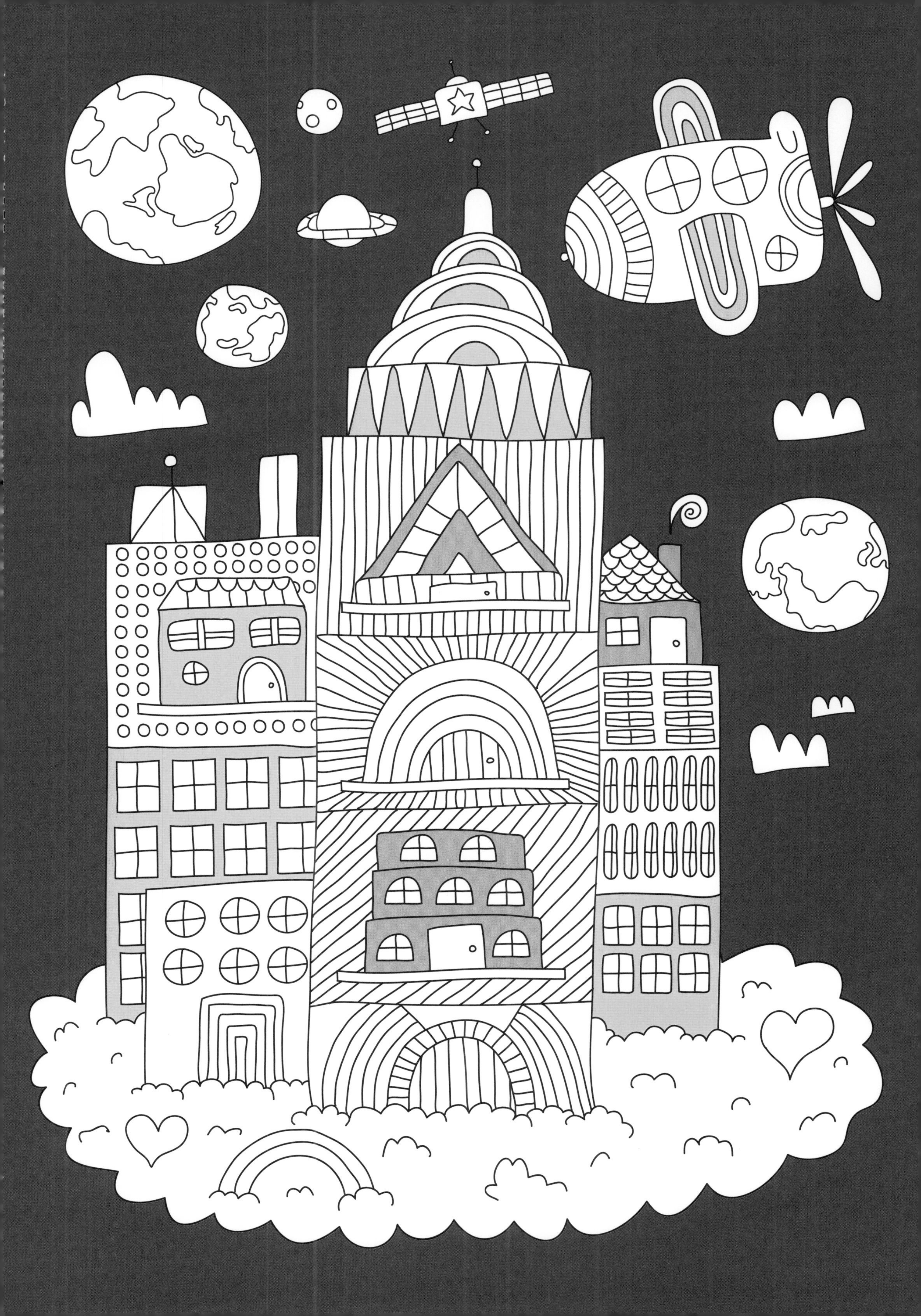

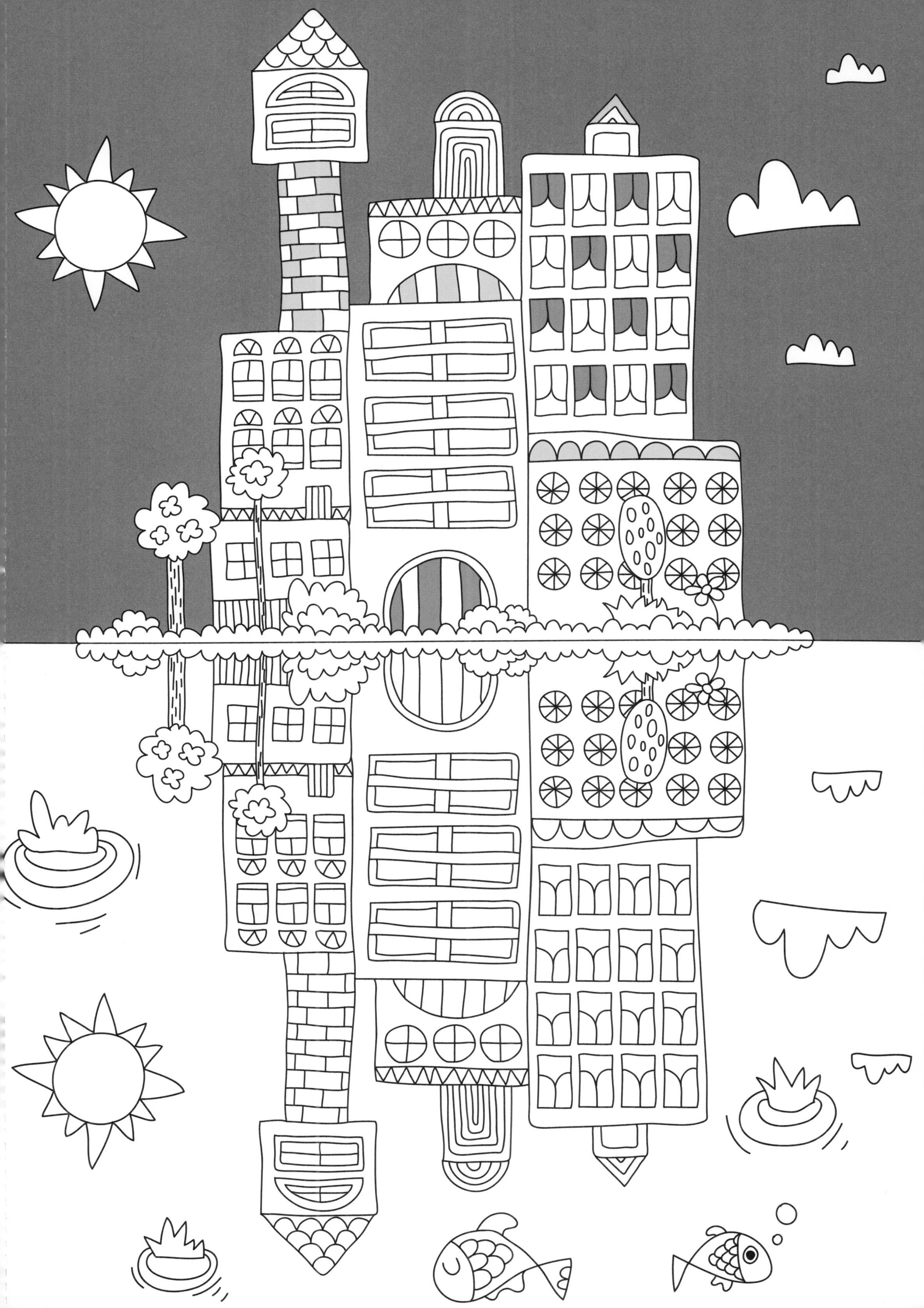

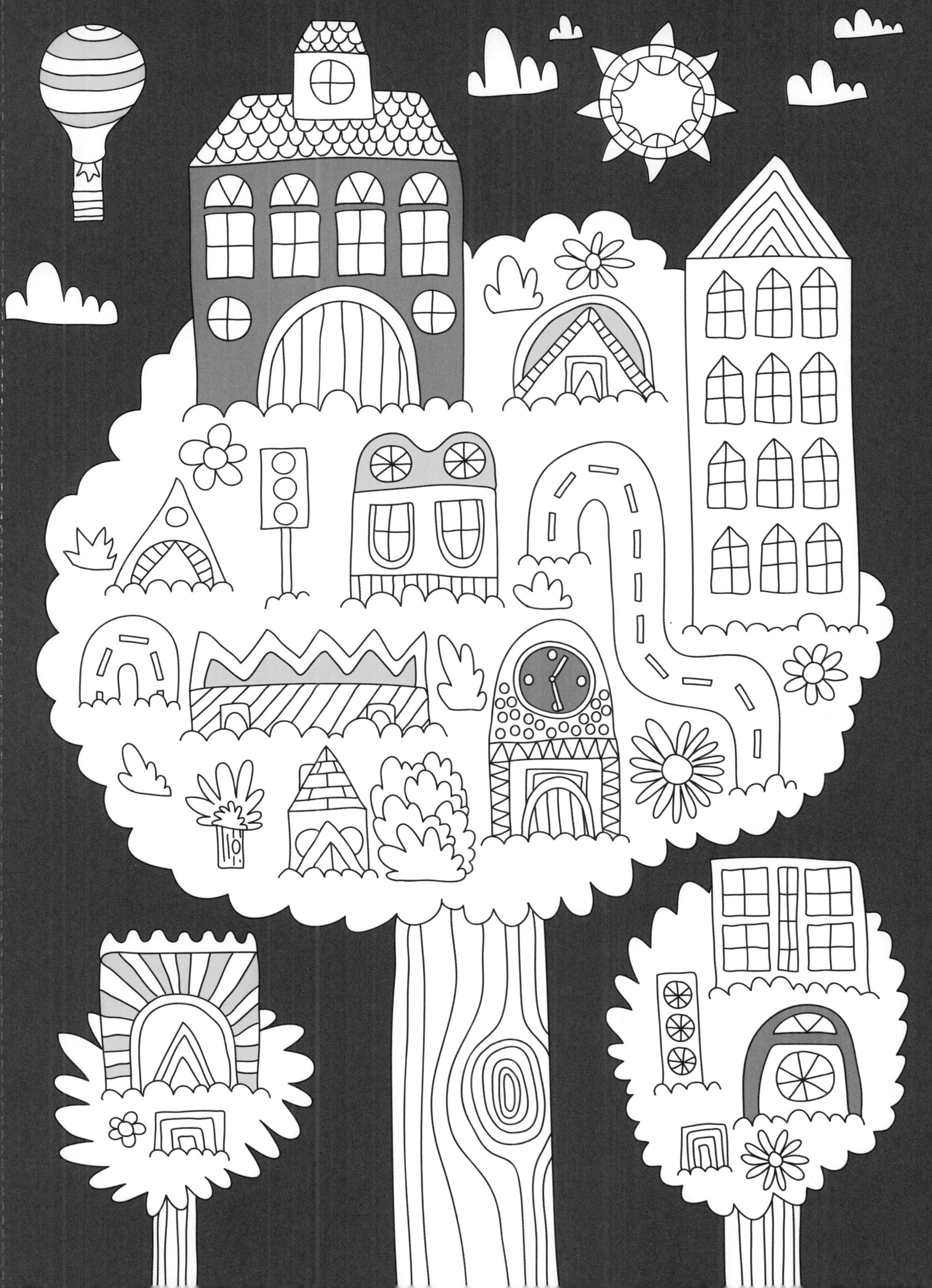

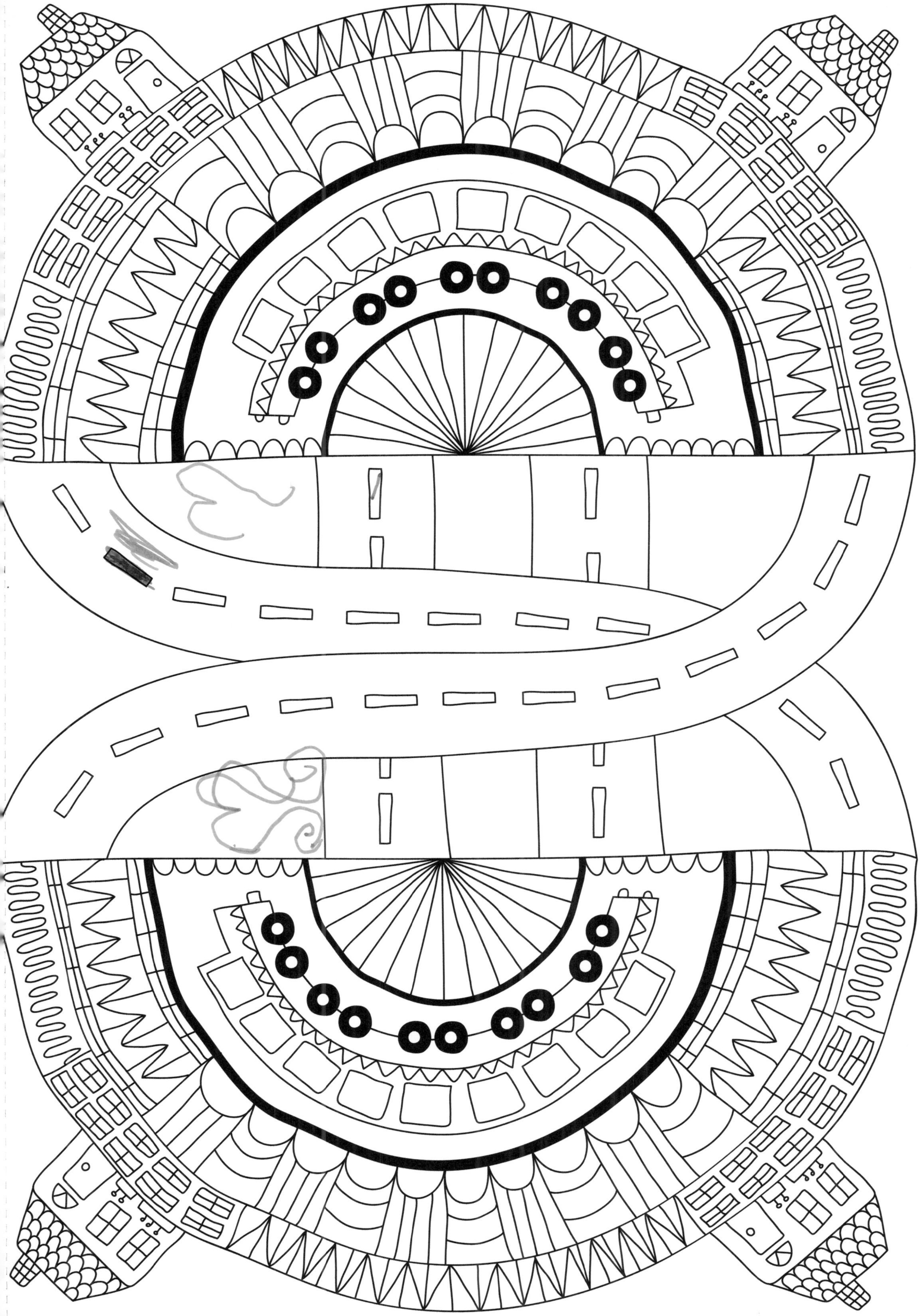

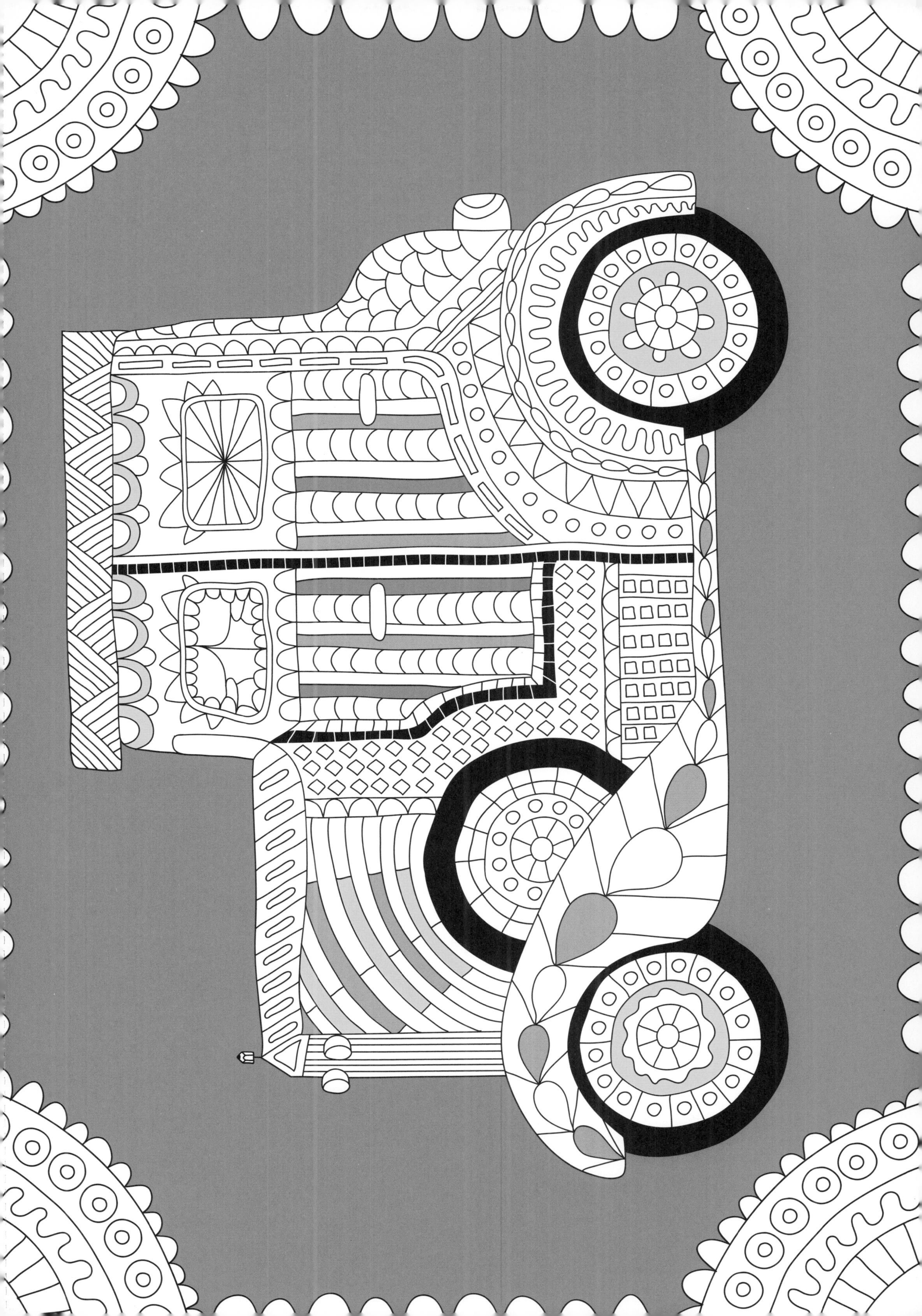

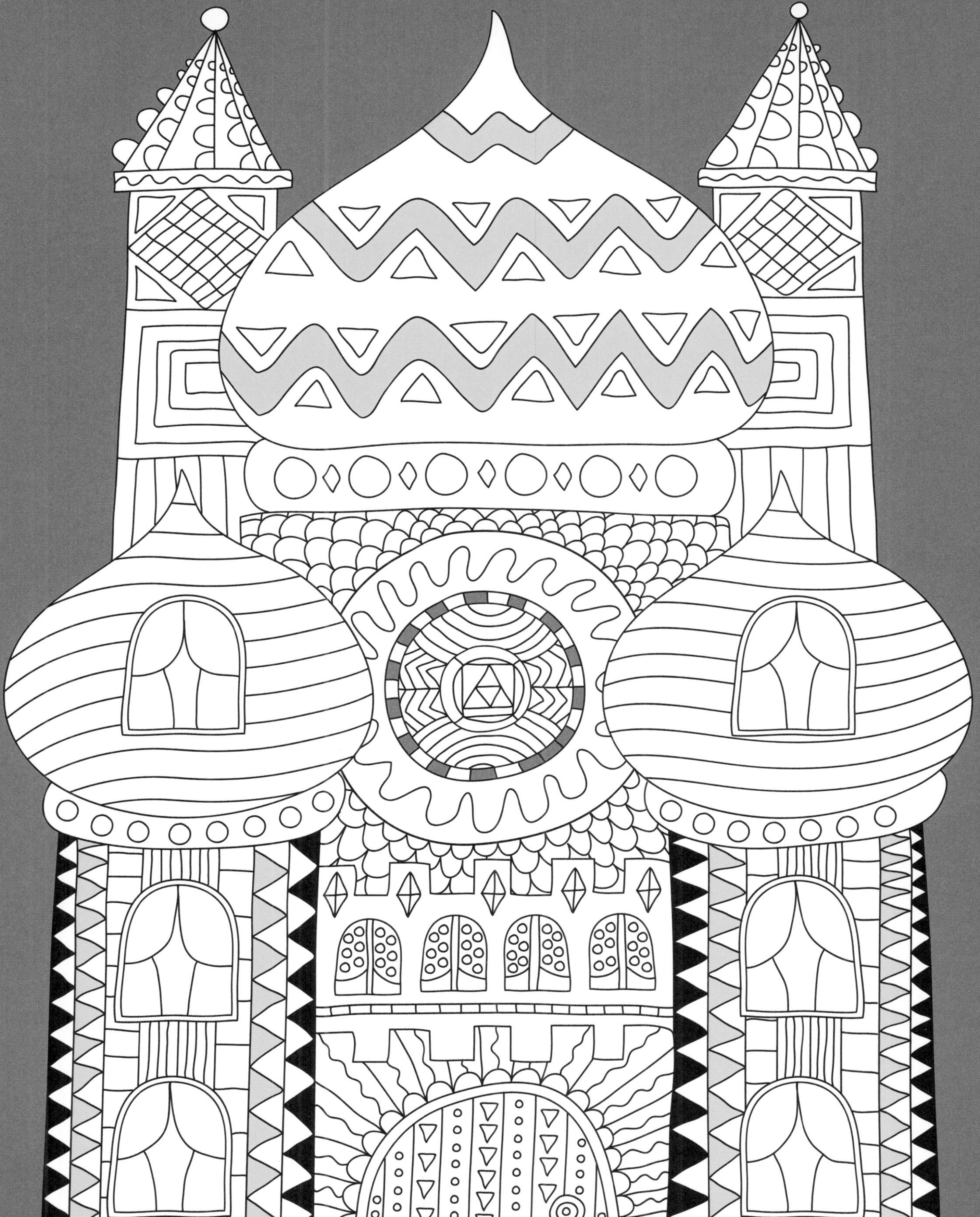

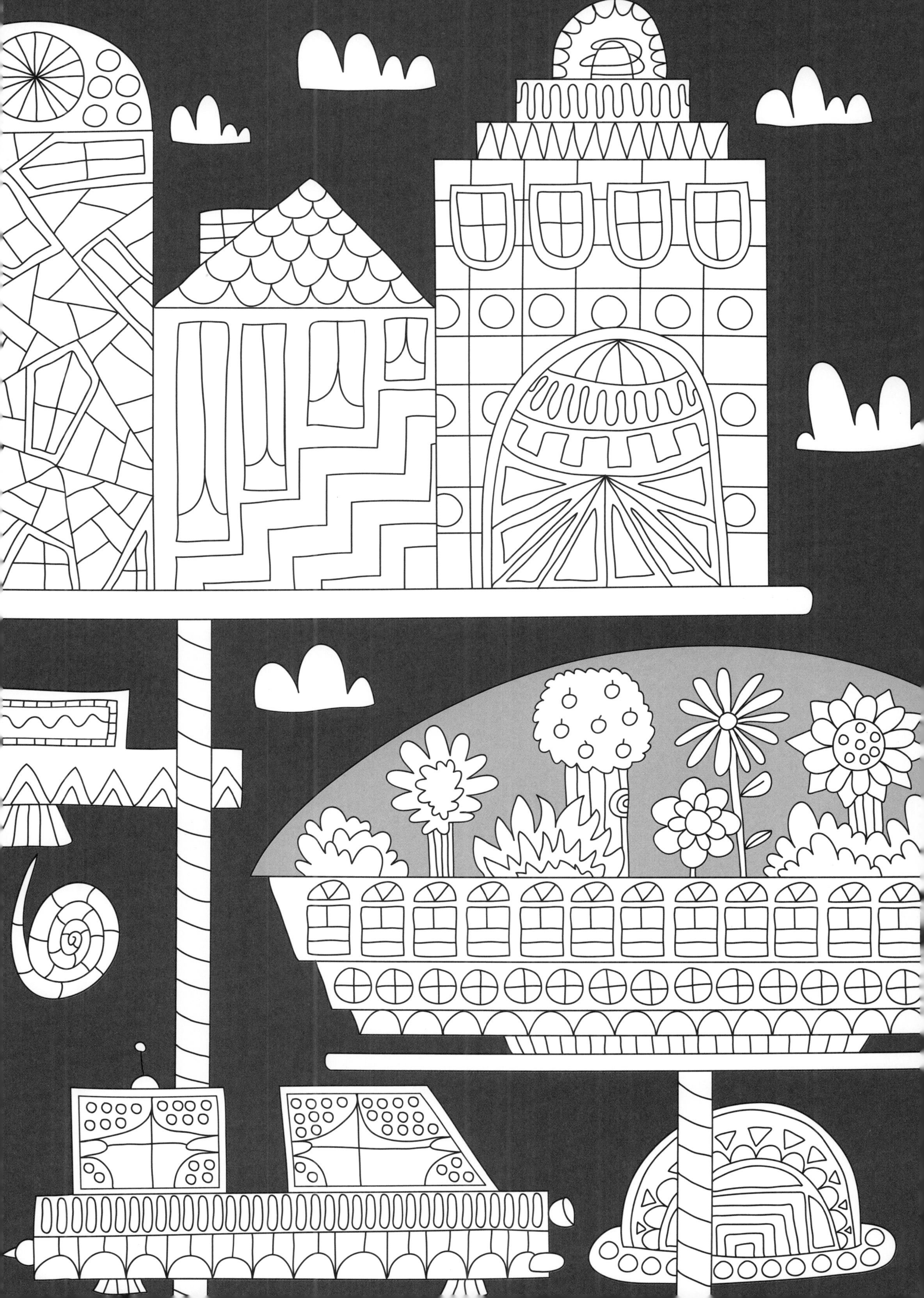